Inside NVLm 1.0

The Multimodal Model That's Changing the Tech Game

How Nvidia's Revolutionary Breakthrough

Combines Vision, Text, and

Problem-Solving to Shape the Future of AI

Kylan P.crook

TABLE OF CONTENT

Introduction: Unveiling NVLM 1.0

Nvidia has always been at the forefront of technological advancement, particularly in the world of artificial intelligence (AI). A company that began as a graphics processing unit (GPU) manufacturer has evolved into one of the most influential players in AI development. From powering cutting-edge video games to driving the deep learning revolution, Nvidia's technology has not only shaped how we interact with the digital world but also pushed the boundaries of what artificial intelligence can achieve.

As AI continues to evolve, Nvidia remains a beacon of innovation, constantly striving to build the next big leap. This brings us to NVLM 1.0, a model that has captured the tech world's imagination, poised to set new standards and redefine what AI can do.

Understanding Nvidia's role in AI innovation requires a look back at some of the company's key milestones. Nvidia's initial contributions to the AI space were mainly through its GPUs, which became the backbone for training deep neural networks. The advent of CUDA, Nvidia's parallel computing platform, enabled developers to harness the full potential of their GPUs for AI tasks, marking the beginning of a new era in machine learning. Over the years, Nvidia has continued to expand its AI portfolio, introducing hardware and software solutions like the DGX systems, TensorRT, and the powerful Omniverse platform for AI simulation.

Each step has paved the way for more complex, efficient, and scalable AI models, and NVLM 1.0 is the latest in this series of groundbreaking developments.

The release of NVLM 1.0 marks a significant milestone in Nvidia's journey, not just because it is another multimodal model, but because it breaks new ground in the way AI processes and integrates information.

NVLM 1.0 is a next-generation model designed to handle both text and visual data simultaneously, a feat that has long been a challenge in AI. What makes this model so extraordinary is its ability to improve across both modalities without compromising on the quality of either. The capabilities of NVLM 1.0 have captured the attention of AI researchers, business leaders, and developers alike, as it opens the door to a new era of AI applications. This model doesn't just enhance what AI can do; it transforms the possibilities, showing us that AI can be both a specialist and a generalist, excelling in multiple areas simultaneously.

The purpose of this book is to explore NVLM 1.0 in detail, offering a comprehensive understanding of why this model is so groundbreaking. It's not just about appreciating the technical specifications of NVLM 1.0; it's about understanding the ripple effects its release will have on the future of AI development.

Why is this model so important? Because it signals a shift in the way AI models are designed and deployed. The ability of NVLM 1.0 to seamlessly handle both text and vision tasks without sacrificing performance in either area challenges conventional wisdom about AI development. This is the kind of breakthrough that could spark innovation across a wide range of industries, from healthcare and finance to entertainment and beyond.

For those who are passionate about AI and its potential, NVLM 1.0 represents a crucial development. Whether you are an AI enthusiast eager to learn about the latest advancements, a researcher exploring the cutting-edge of multimodal models, a developer looking to incorporate powerful new tools into your work, or a business leader seeking to understand how AI can drive future growth, this book will guide you through the transformative potential of NVLM 1.0. The insights contained here aim to ignite curiosity and spark fresh ideas, pushing readers to consider the future possibilities of AI in ways they may not have imagined before.

The curiosity-driven exploration of NVLM 1.0 is a journey into the heart of what makes this model so revolutionary. It's not just another AI tool—it's the harbinger of a new era in AI development. This book will break down the technology behind NVLM 1.0, explain its potential applications, and provide a deep dive into why this model is so important for the future of AI. Whether you are a seasoned expert in the field or someone new to the subject, the story of NVLM 1.0 will capture your imagination and inspire you to think differently about the possibilities of artificial intelligence.

As we venture into the details of Nvidia's latest breakthrough, you'll discover how NVLM 1.0 combines advanced machine learning techniques, sophisticated hardware, and innovative design principles to create a model that is not only powerful but also adaptable. The implications of this technology extend far beyond the research lab; NVLM 1.0 is poised to impact everything from business operations to personal computing, revolutionizing the way AI interacts with the world.

The journey ahead is one of discovery, offering a deeper understanding of Nvidia's role in shaping the future of artificial intelligence and the possibilities that NVLM 1.0 opens up for the industry as a whole.

Chapter 1: The Rise of Multimodal AI Models

The Rise of Multimodal AI Models

The development of artificial intelligence has been marked by many notable milestones, but none quite as transformative as the rise of multimodal AI models. Early AI systems, such as rule-based models and early neural networks, were focused primarily on processing text. They were designed to read, analyze, and generate human language. However, these text-only models had limitations—they could understand words but not images, sounds, or other forms of sensory data.

To replicate human understanding, AI needed to expand beyond a single modality. This is where multimodal models came into play.

The Evolution of AI Models

In the early days of AI, models focused exclusively on text were the norm. These models, such as ELIZA, started as simple, rule-based systems that could understand and generate basic sentences. The technology evolved over time, with breakthroughs such as the development of neural networks, which allowed models to process more complex information. As the amount of available data grew, researchers realized that processing only text wasn't enough.

The world didn't operate in isolated data streams, and neither should AI. Humans experience the world through sight, sound, and language, and AI needs to follow suit.

This realization led to the shift toward multimodal models. The first major step toward this was the introduction of systems that could handle both text and images.

The key difference between earlier text-based models and multimodal systems is the ability to combine these two types of data to enhance understanding. Multimodal AI combines text and vision, and even sound in some cases, allowing AI to understand and respond in a way that's more contextually relevant. With this shift, AI moved from being a tool that could process text in isolation to becoming a far more versatile system that could interpret and generate a wide range of outputs.

What Makes Multimodal Models Different?

At its core, the biggest difference between traditional, text-based models and multimodal AI is the ability to process multiple streams of data at once. Traditional models excel at language tasks—everything from translation to summarization. Multimodal models, however, go beyond text and are capable of integrating other types of data, such as images, video, and even audio.

By combining these different forms of input, multimodal models can perform tasks that text-only models can't.

For instance, when an image is paired with text, a multimodal AI can analyze both simultaneously to understand the meaning behind the image and the context provided by the text. This capability has a wide range of applications. In healthcare, AI systems can be trained to analyze X-rays or MRIs alongside medical texts to offer more accurate diagnoses. In education, multimodal AI can create more engaging learning experiences by combining visual aids, instructional videos, and written content. Entertainment and media industries have also adopted multimodal AI to generate more realistic virtual environments, including voice and visual elements that interact seamlessly.

The Importance of Combining Text and Vision in AI Tasks

The combination of text and vision in AI tasks opens up a new world of possibilities. For example, in the world of e-commerce, a multimodal AI could identify a product from a picture and then provide a detailed description based on the product's visual features.

In autonomous vehicles, AI systems rely on the integration of visual inputs (such as cameras and LiDAR) with textual data (such as maps and traffic updates) to make real-time decisions. The ability to combine vision and language allows AI to handle much more complex tasks, which opens doors to new industries and applications that were previously unimaginable.

Moreover, multimodal AI has proven to be highly beneficial in healthcare, where the ability to interpret both medical imaging and patient history is crucial for diagnosing diseases. It can also improve accessibility, making AI systems more capable of serving diverse needs by combining visual, auditory, and textual information to cater to different types of disabilities. The true value of multimodal AI lies in its versatility and the expanded range of tasks it can tackle, which is why it's being integrated across industries.

Key Players in Multimodal AI

As the field of multimodal AI rapidly expands, several companies have made significant strides in the development of multimodal models. Among the top players are GPT-4, LLaMA 3v, and Intern-VL2, each of which has its own strengths and weaknesses in handling multimodal tasks. GPT-4, for instance, is a strong language model but is still limited in its ability to integrate vision as seamlessly as multimodal models like NVLM 1.0.

LLaMA 3v and Intern-VL2 offer impressive capabilities in processing both text and vision, but they still fall short in certain areas like real-time applications or understanding dynamic content.

While these models are indeed powerful, NVLM 1.0 distinguishes itself by offering an unprecedented level of integration between vision and language.

Where other models may struggle to balance both modalities, NVLM 1.0 is designed to handle them simultaneously without compromising performance in either area. This makes it a highly competitive player in the field, offering a solution that bridges the gap between traditional language understanding and cutting-edge computer vision technology.

How NVLM 1.0 Challenges the Industry

Nvidia's NVLM 1.0 is a game-changing development in the field of multimodal AI. Unlike many of its competitors, NVLM 1.0 excels in providing seamless integration between text and vision, allowing it to tackle a wide range of applications that other models can't.

For instance, NVLM 1.0 could be used to create AI-powered content generation tools that take both textual input and visual elements to generate creative content in real-time. It also has the potential to transform industries such as healthcare, where the need for both text and image analysis is crucial. In fields like autonomous driving and robotics, NVLM 1.0's ability to understand and respond to real-world visual and textual data could prove to be an essential tool in improving decision-making and automation.

By offering a more integrated approach to multimodal AI, NVLM 1.0 is not just another step forward in the evolution of AI—it is a leap. It challenges the entire industry to rethink what is possible, and its capabilities point to a future where AI is more versatile, efficient, and adaptable than ever before. With NVLM 1.0 leading the charge, it's clear that the future of AI is multimodal, and the possibilities are just beginning to unfold.

Chapter 2: Deep Dive into NVLM 1.0

Nvidia's NVLM 1.0 has emerged as a groundbreaking multimodal AI model, blending text and vision capabilities in a way that promises to redefine the future of artificial intelligence. Built upon years of research, NVLM 1.0 reflects Nvidia's vision of a more powerful and integrated approach to AI, one that can handle not just language and text, but also visual inputs in a cohesive and efficient manner.

Introduction to NVLM 1.0

At the heart of Nvidia's ambition is NVLM 1.0, an AI model that seeks to break the barriers between visual and textual data. Nvidia has long been a leader in the AI space, developing cutting-edge technologies that power everything from GPUs to AI research. The launch of NVLM 1.0 represents a major milestone in its ongoing mission to push the boundaries of what artificial intelligence can do.

Nvidia's vision behind NVLM 1.0 is clear: to create an AI system that doesn't just process text, or just analyze images, but one that combines both in a way that makes sense for real-world applications. While many AI systems struggle to integrate visual and textual data, NVLM 1.0 merges them seamlessly, creating a model that is far more capable of performing complex tasks like content creation, medical diagnostics, and autonomous decision-making.

Model Architecture: Combining the Best of Decoder-Only and Cross-Attention-Based Designs

NVLM 1.0's architecture is the key to its success. It doesn't rely on just one design paradigm but instead takes the best elements from both decoder-only and cross-attention-based models. The decoder-only architecture allows the model to focus on sequential processing of information, generating language from a given input. Meanwhile, the cross-attention design allows it to handle multiple types of data—whether that's text, image, or other modalities—by associating different parts of the data in a way that makes sense contextually.

By blending these two approaches, NVLM 1.0 can handle a broader range of tasks more effectively than most traditional models. The synergy between these two design philosophies allows the model to handle tasks that would normally require separate systems, offering far more flexibility and a deeper level of understanding.

The hybrid approach also enables NVLM 1.0 to run more efficiently, making it suitable for both research and real-world applications.

Training Methodology and Data Sets

For NVLM 1.0 to be as powerful as it is, its training methodology had to be innovative and comprehensive. Nvidia leveraged vast amounts of diverse data sets, including everything from image databases to text corpora, allowing the model to learn how different types of data interact. By using large-scale data, NVLM 1.0 can understand nuances in both language and visuals, making it highly capable of solving complex problems.

The training process also involved teaching the model how to respond to real-world inputs. This not only included traditional datasets but also involved simulating scenarios where both text and vision data were present. By immersing the model in these rich, multimodal experiences, Nvidia ensured that NVLM 1.0 wouldn't just be a theoretical advancement—it would be a model with practical, real-world applications.

What Makes NVLM 1.0 Revolutionary?

NVLM 1.0 is revolutionary because it can seamlessly integrate tasks that were once isolated to different AI systems. By combining language processing with image recognition, it can perform complex operations that require deep understanding of both types of data simultaneously. This capability is game-changing, especially when it comes to real-world applications like medical imaging, e-commerce, and autonomous vehicles.

One key capability that sets NVLM 1.0 apart is its ability to perform Optical Character Recognition (OCR) directly on images, extracting text from pictures or scanned documents. This can be incredibly valuable in industries like logistics, healthcare, and finance, where images or scanned documents are part of daily operations.

NVLM 1.0's ability to handle OCR within the same model that processes visual data makes it a highly efficient solution.

Moreover, NVLM 1.0 excels at problem-solving tasks. Whether it's answering questions based on a given image or generating descriptive captions for complex visual scenarios, the model can tackle problem-solving tasks with a high degree of accuracy. This combination of vision and language capabilities positions NVLM 1.0 as a truly revolutionary tool, pushing the boundaries of what AI systems can do.

Notable Improvements Over Competitors: GPT-4, LLaMA 3v, etc.

Compared to competitors like GPT-4, LLaMA 3v, and others, NVLM 1.0 shows a noticeable leap forward in terms of integration and versatility. While GPT-4 is a strong language model, it falls short in terms of vision capabilities, making it less suitable for tasks requiring an understanding of both text and images. LLaMA 3v, on the other hand, has made strides in multimodal capabilities, but NVLM 1.0 outshines it with its seamless integration of language and vision data.

NVLM 1.0 is designed to perform at a level where both modalities—text and vision—are treated equally, rather than as separate entities, which is what often happens in competing models. This makes NVLM 1.0 far more capable of handling complex, real-world applications, from autonomous vehicles to AI-driven customer service, in a way that GPT-4 or LLaMA 3v can't match.

Architectural Innovations

One of the most notable architectural innovations of NVLM 1.0 is its hybrid design. By fusing the strengths of decoder-only and cross-attention-based models, Nvidia has created a system that doesn't just process information in one modality or the other.

Instead, it allows for the seamless processing of both types of data in parallel, resulting in a more cohesive and intelligent model.

Another architectural innovation is the tile tagging design, which significantly improves how the model handles visual data. This system divides images into smaller segments or "tiles" and tags them with relevant information, making it easier for the model to process and interpret images in greater detail. The tile tagging design improves the efficiency and accuracy of visual data processing, ensuring that NVLM 1.0 can handle even the most complex visual tasks with ease.

Importance of High-Resolution Image Processing in Real-World Applications

In real-world applications, especially those in fields like healthcare and autonomous driving, high-resolution image processing is vital. NVLM 1.0 is capable of analyzing images at a high resolution, allowing it to interpret fine details that may be crucial for accurate decision-making. Whether it's scanning a high-resolution medical image for signs of disease or interpreting complex street scenes for an autonomous vehicle, NVLM 1.0's ability to process high-resolution images sets it apart from competitors. This makes the model more versatile, reliable, and ready for real-world applications.

In conclusion, NVLM 1.0 stands out as a significant advancement in the world of multimodal AI. By combining innovative architectural designs, advanced training methodologies, and a focus on real-world applications, NVLM 1.0 is positioning itself as a leader in the AI space. Its ability to seamlessly integrate vision and language tasks makes it not just an AI model, but a powerful tool that can change the way we interact with technology and solve complex problems.

Chapter 3: Performance Benchmarks and Real-World Applications

---

NVLM 1.0 stands out in the field of artificial intelligence not just because of its theoretical advancements but also due to its exceptional performance on a wide range of real-world tasks. These benchmarks offer a glimpse into how the model performs under real-world conditions and compare its efficiency and capabilities to other leading models in the industry. Through various performance metrics, NVLM 1.0 has proven to be a top-tier solution, pushing the boundaries of what AI can do across multiple domains.

Industry-Leading Benchmark Results

NVLM 1.0 has achieved remarkable success across several key industry-standard benchmarks, confirming its position as a next-generation multimodal AI system. Notably, its performance on Optical Character Recognition (OCR) Bench, Visual Question Answering (VQA), MathVista, DocVQA, and others is exceptional. These benchmarks are designed to test various aspects of AI, from reading and interpreting text within images to solving complex mathematical problems or answering questions based on visual data.

In OCR Bench, NVLM 1.0 has surpassed expectations by demonstrating superior accuracy in extracting text from both printed and handwritten documents, outshining previous models like GPT-4 and LLaMA 3v. This capability is particularly significant for industries where document digitization is critical, such as healthcare, finance, and legal services.

Furthermore, in VQA, which tests the model's ability to answer questions based on visual inputs, NVLM 1.0 outperforms its competitors, making it a reliable option for applications requiring deep understanding of visual contexts.

NVLM 1.0 also performed exceptionally well in MathVista, a benchmark that tests AI's ability to solve complex mathematical problems from visual data. In comparison to other models that struggle with mathematical reasoning, NVLM 1.0's problem-solving capabilities set a new standard for multimodal AI. Lastly, DocVQA tested NVLM 1.0's ability to comprehend documents and extract relevant information based on visual cues, where the model's cross-modal efficiency truly shines.

Breaking Down Key Tasks and Achievements

NVLM 1.0's performance is not just impressive in aggregate but also stands out across key tasks that test the model's core capabilities.

The following sections break down these tasks and achievements, showcasing the full potential of this powerful AI system.

Optical Character Recognition (OCR)

One of NVLM 1.0's standout features is its ability to perform high-accuracy OCR, which involves extracting textual information from images or scanned documents. The model goes beyond simply reading printed text—its hybrid design enables it to recognize and interpret handwritten text, no matter the quality or form of the input. This capability has vast implications in sectors like healthcare, where doctors and hospitals still deal with an immense amount of handwritten medical records, prescriptions, and patient notes. NVLM 1.0 can easily digitize these documents, saving both time and resources.

Moreover, its advanced OCR performance helps automate data entry tasks, reducing human error and accelerating workflows in industries like finance and logistics, where processing large volumes of documents is routine. By accurately converting various forms of visual text into usable data, NVLM 1.0 supports faster, more accurate decision-making across multiple fields.

Visual Question Answering (VQA)

Visual Question Answering (VQA) is a task that combines language understanding with image recognition to answer questions based on visual inputs. NVLM 1.0 excels in this area, achieving high accuracy in responding to complex, context-based questions. Whether it's identifying objects in images or understanding the relationship between various elements in a picture, NVLM 1.0 can handle a wide range of questions that require not only visual comprehension but also reasoning.

This capability is invaluable in fields such as e-commerce, where AI-powered systems can assist customers by identifying products in images and answering specific questions about those products.

Additionally, in industries like education and healthcare, where analyzing visual data and providing accurate answers is critical, NVLM 1.0's VQA abilities are a game-changer. For example, it can assist doctors by analyzing medical images and answering questions about a patient's condition based on the visual data.

Math and Coding Problem-Solving Capabilities

In areas like math and coding, NVLM 1.0 takes on challenges that few other AI models can manage. MathVista, a benchmark for solving visual math problems, tests the model's ability to solve complex problems presented in visual formats. Unlike traditional models that struggle with understanding and solving mathematical problems from images, NVLM 1.0 uses its hybrid architecture to not only interpret the visual elements but also to understand the mathematical concepts behind them.

NVLM 1.0 can decode word problems, equations, and visual representations of data, providing accurate solutions to questions. This capability has profound implications in sectors like education, where AI can help students by solving problems interactively, or in fields like finance, where solving visual-based financial reports or calculations can be crucial.

Furthermore, NVLM 1.0's coding problem-solving abilities make it an asset to developers and coders. The model can understand programming languages, debug code, and even provide insights into the development of complex software systems, marking a significant advancement over traditional coding AIs that only offer limited functionalities.

Document and Image-Based Reasoning Tasks

NVLM 1.0 also performs exceptionally well in document and image-based reasoning tasks, which require the AI to make logical inferences based on the data it processes. This capability is critical in industries where understanding and processing documents and images are paramount to success. Whether it's interpreting legal documents, analyzing product catalogs, or assessing blueprints in construction, NVLM 1.0 can offer more detailed insights and automated reasoning than most competing models.

For example, in the legal industry, NVLM 1.0 can help lawyers by analyzing contracts, identifying potential risks, and extracting relevant clauses and conditions. In healthcare, the model can assist in analyzing medical imaging and diagnostic reports, providing quicker insights into patient conditions and treatment options.

Real-World Use Cases and Impact

The true power of NVLM 1.0, however, lies in its real-world applications. Here, the model is not just an academic exercise or a theoretical breakthrough—it is transforming industries and providing practical solutions to challenges faced by businesses, educators, healthcare providers, and more.

Healthcare: Analyzing Medical Records and Digitizing Data

In the healthcare industry, NVLM 1.0 can scan and interpret medical records, X-rays, MRI scans, and other visual data. With its OCR and image-based reasoning capabilities, it helps doctors and healthcare professionals digitize patient records, extract key information from medical images, and even assist in diagnosis. This streamlines administrative tasks and improves accuracy in clinical decision-making, all while saving valuable time in patient care.

Education: Interactive Problem-Solving and Personalized Learning

In education, NVLM 1.0 serves as a dynamic tool for interactive learning. It can assist students in solving complex math and science problems, offer real-time feedback, and help personalize learning experiences based on individual needs. Its ability to process both visual and textual data allows it to create engaging and effective learning modules for students, making education more accessible and tailored to each learner's pace and style.

Business: Automating Invoice and Receipt Processing in Finance

For businesses, particularly in finance, NVLM 1.0 can automate invoice and receipt processing, reducing human intervention in routine but important tasks. The model's ability to understand both the visual data (scanned invoices, receipts) and the textual content (payment terms, amounts) makes it invaluable for automating accounts payable and receivable. This reduces the risk of errors, speeds up processing time, and allows businesses to allocate resources more efficiently.

Content Creation: Enhancing Advertising and Creative Writing

In the realm of content creation, NVLM 1.0 offers significant enhancements. It can generate creative writing pieces, suggest content ideas, and even help design advertisements based on both textual input and visual themes. By analyzing both text and images, NVLM 1.0 can create more targeted, personalized content for marketers and creatives, pushing the boundaries of AI-driven creativity.

Through these real-world applications, NVLM 1.0 is not just shaping the future of AI—it's already impacting industries, improving efficiency, and opening new avenues for innovation. Its performance benchmarks and real-world use cases make it clear: NVLM 1.0 is poised to change the way we think about artificial intelligence and its capabilities in everyday life.

Chapter 4: NVLM 1.0 vs. The Competition: A Close Look

The world of artificial intelligence is evolving at an unprecedented pace, and models like NVLM 1.0 are playing a crucial role in shaping the direction of the industry. As AI continues to push the boundaries of what's possible, the competition between models like NVLM 1.0 and its contemporaries becomes more intense. Understanding where NVLM 1.0 stands in relation to other leading AI models is essential for grasping its significance and potential.

Understanding the AI Race

NVLM 1.0 enters a rapidly developing field where performance and versatility are paramount. Its ability to seamlessly integrate both text and vision tasks positions it as one of the most advanced AI models available today.

But in a crowded field, NVLM 1.0 isn't just competing for supremacy in the market—it's setting new standards for what AI can achieve across a variety of domains, from visual reasoning to text comprehension, and even problem-solving.

The AI space is evolving from models that excel in one specific area to systems that can handle a broader range of tasks. NVLM 1.0 stands out in this transition, offering a unique combination of abilities. Its performance across text, vision, and problem-solving is notable for its consistency and adaptability, making it a serious contender in the AI race.

A key advantage of NVLM 1.0 is its ability to perform at a high level in both traditional text-based tasks (such as natural language processing and text generation) and visually-based tasks (like image recognition and optical character recognition). This broad capability is what makes NVLM 1.0 so compelling—it does not require specialized models for different tasks but instead integrates them into a single, cohesive system.

A Closer Look at Key Competitors

In order to truly appreciate NVLM 1.0's position in the AI landscape, it's crucial to examine its key competitors. Each of these models has its own strengths and weaknesses, which highlights NVLM 1.0's unique approach to multimodal AI.

GPT-4: Overview and Areas of Competition

GPT-4, developed by OpenAI, is one of the most advanced language models in the world. It is highly sophisticated when it comes to text generation and understanding, capable of producing high-quality writing, answering questions, and engaging in complex conversations. However, GPT-4's capabilities are primarily centered around text—it is not designed for processing visual data.

While it can understand images through external tools like image captioning, it does not have the same seamless integration of visual and textual tasks that NVLM 1.0 boasts.

NVLM 1.0 has an edge over GPT-4 in its multimodal design. The model's ability to handle both text and vision tasks with equal efficiency means it can tackle more complex, real-world scenarios where both types of data are required. For example, in industries like healthcare, GPT-4 might be able to analyze patient records and provide natural language summaries, but NVLM 1.0 can also process medical images like X-rays, making it a more versatile solution for medical professionals who require both text and visual data to make informed decisions.

LLaMA 3v: Strengths and Weaknesses

LLaMA 3v, developed by Meta, is another competitor that has drawn attention in the field of multimodal AI.

Like NVLM 1.0, LLaMA 3v is designed to handle both text and vision-based tasks, but its performance has been mixed. On the one hand, LLaMA 3v excels in language processing, and its text-based outputs can be as strong as GPT-4's. However, when it comes to integrating visual data with text, LLaMA 3v does not perform at the same level of proficiency as NVLM 1.0.

The main challenge for LLaMA 3v lies in its ability to manage and process high-resolution visual data. NVLM 1.0's hybrid architecture, with tile-tagging and cross-attention mechanisms, allows it to process visual data at a much higher level of detail and accuracy than LLaMA 3v. Additionally, while LLaMA 3v can handle basic image recognition tasks, it often struggles with complex tasks that require advanced reasoning across text and visual elements, a strength of NVLM 1.0.

Intern-VL2: Comparative Analysis

Intern-VL2, developed by Baidu, is another important player in the multimodal AI space. This model focuses on the intersection of text and vision, and like NVLM 1.0, it is designed to handle complex visual reasoning tasks alongside text generation. However, while Intern-VL2 is a strong model in its own right, it lacks the level of integration and consistency that NVLM 1.0 offers.

Intern-VL2's performance in tasks like visual question answering (VQA) and document analysis is competitive, but its reliance on a purely vision-based design can sometimes limit its flexibility. NVLM 1.0's ability to seamlessly handle both vision and language tasks, combined with its advanced problem-solving capabilities, makes it a more balanced and reliable option for real-world applications.

NVLM 1.0's Advantages

NVLM 1.0 is unique because it addresses the common limitations of previous multimodal models.

One of the main challenges with many multimodal systems is the trade-off between handling visual and textual tasks. Many models perform well in one area but struggle in the other, or they fail to consistently maintain performance across both tasks. NVLM 1.0, however, manages to avoid these trade-offs, offering exceptional performance across both domains without sacrificing efficiency.

Its architectural innovations, including the tile-tagging design for enhanced visual data processing and the hybrid approach to integrating text and vision, provide a level of consistency that is difficult to find in other AI models. This means that NVLM 1.0 can perform equally well in complex tasks that involve both text and images, such as interpreting medical scans while providing detailed patient records, or processing invoices while generating business insights.

Another advantage of NVLM 1.0 is its ability to scale. Whether dealing with simple text-based tasks or more complex image and document-based challenges, the model's versatility ensures that it can handle a wide range of real-world applications without needing specialized systems for each task. This consistency across tasks positions NVLM 1.0 as a more practical solution for businesses and organizations seeking a powerful, all-in-one AI system.

The Future of AI Models: Specialized vs. Generalized AI

Looking ahead, NVLM 1.0's versatility raises important questions about the future of AI models. Will specialized models—those designed to excel in specific tasks, like GPT-4 for text generation or LLaMA 3v for image recognition—continue to dominate, or will generalized models, like NVLM 1.0, become the new standard?

NVLM 1.0's success suggests that generalized models will play an increasingly important role in AI's future. The ability to handle both text and vision without sacrificing performance in either area makes NVLM 1.0 a powerful tool in industries where complex, multimodal data is the norm. As AI systems become more integrated into everyday life, the demand for these generalized models is likely to grow, with NVLM 1.0 at the forefront of this shift.

Implications for Future AI Model Development

NVLM 1.0's performance and capabilities have significant implications for the future of AI model development. The model's success demonstrates that hybrid, multimodal AI systems can outperform traditional models that specialize in one task.

As more industries adopt AI solutions, models like NVLM 1.0 will likely set the standard for what is possible in AI, offering a glimpse into a future where AI systems are more capable, more efficient, and more accessible than ever before.

In conclusion, while NVLM 1.0 faces competition from other advanced AI models, its seamless integration of text and vision, combined with its consistent performance and innovative architecture, make it a standout in the field. As the AI race continues to evolve, NVLM 1.0's strengths in multimodal tasks may very well redefine what's possible for AI systems, opening up new possibilities and applications across industries.

Chapter 5: Nvidia's Open-Source Revolution

In an era where technology continues to evolve at breakneck speeds, open-source initiatives have become one of the driving forces behind innovation. The power of open-source software lies in its ability to democratize access to advanced technologies, enabling anyone—regardless of resources or geographical location—to contribute, experiment, and improve. Nvidia, a leader in AI research and development, has taken this philosophy to heart with the release of NVLM 1.0.

By making its cutting-edge multimodal model available to the open-source community, Nvidia is not just advancing AI capabilities, but also catalyzing a broader revolution in the way artificial intelligence is developed, accessed, and applied.

Open Source and Its Impact

The significance of open-source AI in the tech community cannot be overstated. Open-source software, by its very nature, removes barriers to entry for individuals and organizations seeking to explore advanced technologies. In the realm of AI, where resources like computational power and high-quality data can be prohibitively expensive, open-source models allow researchers and developers to access state-of-the-art tools without needing massive infrastructure or funding. This level of access fosters a culture of collaboration, knowledge-sharing, and rapid iteration, all of which are essential to the fast-paced world of AI development.

Nvidia's decision to make NVLM 1.0 open-source represents a landmark shift in the AI landscape.

By releasing the model under an open-source license, Nvidia is not only giving the global AI community access to an incredibly powerful tool, but also promoting a sense of transparency and trust in the development process. Traditionally, cutting-edge AI models have been closely guarded by tech giants, with access limited to a select few researchers, developers, or organizations. But NVLM 1.0's open-source nature means that anyone—from independent developers to large corporations—can experiment with, modify, and build upon the model.

This move is poised to have far-reaching implications. The most immediate impact is the ability to accelerate innovation. With NVLM 1.0 being publicly available, the AI community can rapidly build upon its capabilities, identify areas for improvement, and apply it to a broader array of industries and tasks.

The flow of contributions and improvements will likely push the boundaries of what is possible, creating a feedback loop where the technology improves faster than ever before.

What Does Open-Source Mean for Researchers and Developers?

For researchers, the open-source release of NVLM 1.0 is a game-changer. Rather than starting from scratch or relying on proprietary models, researchers can now use NVLM 1.0 as a foundation for their own work. This means they can focus on solving specific challenges or exploring new applications without being hindered by the limitations of closed-source systems. Researchers can test NVLM 1.0's capabilities on various datasets, tailor the model to address niche problems, and fine-tune it for unique applications—whether in healthcare, education, or entertainment.

The freedom to modify and experiment with NVLM 1.0 opens up a world of possibilities for new AI applications.

Imagine a researcher focused on developing AI for disaster response: by tweaking NVLM 1.0, they could train the model to analyze satellite imagery and textual reports simultaneously, improving the model's ability to respond to emergencies in real time. Similarly, AI applications in the legal field could benefit from the model's ability to process both written contracts and accompanying images (such as legal charts or evidence).

But the benefits of open-source AI extend beyond just the academic community. Startups and independent developers now have the opportunity to build their own AI solutions on top of NVLM 1.0's powerful capabilities. These smaller companies, who may not have the resources to develop their own multimodal models from the ground up, can leverage NVLM 1.0 to create innovative products that were previously out of reach. For instance, a small business could use NVLM 1.0 to develop an AI tool for automatic invoice processing or customer support chatbots that not only understand text but can also analyze images (such as scanned receipts or product photos).

The shift in accessibility that comes with an open-source model like NVLM 1.0 is also important for smaller companies and independent developers. These groups are often sidelined by the resources of larger corporations. Yet, by utilizing open-source models, they can bring powerful AI technologies into their products without having to compete with giants for proprietary solutions. In this way, Nvidia's open-source initiative is lowering the barriers to entry for a whole new generation of developers and businesses.

It encourages diversity in innovation and provides opportunities for new voices to emerge in the AI field.

Megatron Core: The Platform Behind NVLM 1.0

One of the most exciting aspects of NVLM 1.0's open-source release is its integration with Megatron Core, Nvidia's robust platform designed for training and deploying large AI models. Megatron Core simplifies the process of working with advanced AI models like NVLM 1.0, making it easier for developers to access, implement, and fine-tune these powerful tools. With Megatron Core, researchers and developers can easily tap into NVLM 1.0's capabilities without needing to build their own infrastructure from the ground up.

Megatron Core is a platform that enables distributed training, meaning that it can leverage multiple GPUs (graphics processing units) to speed up the training process for large models.

This is crucial for NVLM 1.0, given the size and complexity of the multimodal data it processes. Rather than requiring a single, massive GPU to handle all the heavy lifting, Megatron Core allows users to distribute the workload across multiple units, significantly reducing the time and resources needed for training.

Additionally, Megatron Core provides a set of tools and resources that further facilitate the process of working with NVLM 1.0. These include pre-built training pipelines, documentation, and support for various machine learning frameworks. Whether developers are looking to run quick experiments or build large-scale applications, Megatron Core ensures that NVLM 1.0 is accessible to a wide range of users.

The platform's scalability and flexibility also mean that it can accommodate developers with varying levels of expertise.

A seasoned AI researcher with access to a high-performance computing setup may use Megatron Core to train models at an advanced scale, while a smaller startup or independent developer can still use the platform to fine-tune a pre-trained model and deploy it on a cloud-based system. This versatility makes Megatron Core an essential tool for those looking to harness the power of NVLM 1.0.

Tools and Resources Available for Innovation

Beyond just providing the infrastructure for running NVLM 1.0, Nvidia has also developed a suite of tools to empower developers to innovate with the model. These resources are designed to make it easier for users to experiment, customize, and create novel applications using NVLM 1.0.

Nvidia's AI tools for NVLM 1.0 include software libraries that support everything from model optimization to data preprocessing.

These libraries can be used to enhance the model's performance in specific domains, enabling developers to refine NVLM 1.0 for niche tasks. Additionally, tools for integrating NVLM 1.0 with existing systems—whether for commercial applications or academic research—are readily available. By offering these tools, Nvidia is enabling developers to seamlessly integrate NVLM 1.0 into their existing workflows and projects.

For AI entrepreneurs and startups, Nvidia's ecosystem provides additional support, including access to a network of collaborators, funding opportunities, and business development resources. By fostering a strong community around NVLM 1.0, Nvidia is helping to create an environment where innovation thrives and new applications of AI can be discovered faster than ever before.

Nvidia's decision to open-source NVLM 1.0 is a pivotal moment in the AI industry.

By making this advanced multimodal model accessible to a global community of developers, researchers, and businesses, Nvidia is helping to catalyze a new wave of AI innovation.

The ability to integrate NVLM 1.0 into a wide range of applications—coupled with the power of Megatron Core and other Nvidia tools—empowers developers to explore new frontiers in artificial intelligence. As more users contribute to its development, NVLM 1.0 will continue to evolve and shape the future of AI, enabling applications that are more powerful, more flexible, and more impactful than ever before.

Chapter 6: How NVLM 1.0 is Reshaping Industries

As the digital transformation accelerates across various sectors, artificial intelligence continues to make a profound impact, with its applications expanding into areas once thought to be reserved for human ingenuity. NVLM 1.0, Nvidia's groundbreaking multimodal model, is at the forefront of this revolution, providing solutions that integrate text, vision, and problem-solving in ways that are reshaping industries. Its ability to analyze and process both text and visual data simultaneously makes it a versatile tool, unlocking new possibilities and enabling businesses to streamline operations, enhance customer experiences, and create innovative products and services.

Let's explore how NVLM 1.0 is transforming key industries: healthcare, education, finance, and entertainment.

Healthcare: From Medical Imaging to Data Processing

The healthcare industry has been one of the most dynamic sectors in adopting AI, with technologies like machine learning and computer vision improving diagnostics, treatment plans, and patient care. NVLM 1.0's ability to process both textual data and visual information, such as medical images, is playing a pivotal role in transforming healthcare practices. Medical professionals are now able to harness the power of multimodal AI to improve accuracy, efficiency, and speed in the analysis of health data.

Practical applications in health data analysis are numerous. For instance, NVLM 1.0 can be used to process large volumes of patient records, including handwritten notes, scanned reports, and diagnostic images, such as X-rays and MRIs. By combining these sources of information, the model can detect patterns and correlations that would be challenging for humans to uncover, providing doctors with deeper insights into patient conditions. The result is faster diagnoses and more informed decision-making.

In addition to data analysis, NVLM 1.0's ability to automate diagnostic processes is revolutionizing patient care. For example, the model can analyze medical images to identify early signs of diseases like cancer, heart conditions, or neurological disorders, providing healthcare professionals with an early warning system. It can also assist in automated triage systems, helping prioritize patients based on the severity of their conditions.

As the healthcare sector moves toward precision medicine, NVLM 1.0 is providing the tools necessary to make personalized treatment plans a reality, potentially improving patient outcomes and reducing medical costs.

Education: Transforming Learning and Tutoring

Education is another sector where NVLM 1.0 is leaving a lasting imprint. With the rapid shift towards digital learning platforms, there has been a growing demand for tools that can offer personalized learning experiences, adapt to students' needs, and facilitate interactive teaching. NVLM 1.0 is addressing these challenges by making learning more dynamic, engaging, and tailored to individual students' abilities and preferences.

In interactive learning environments, NVLM 1.0 enables a more immersive and responsive experience. The model can process both text-based content, such as textbooks or articles, and visual data, like diagrams, infographics, and videos, making it an ideal tool for modern educational applications.

For instance, in subjects like history or biology, where a combination of textual and visual learning materials is crucial, NVLM 1.0 can offer contextualized explanations by analyzing both types of content. This allows students to gain a deeper understanding of the subject matter, as the model can integrate different types of learning materials into a cohesive lesson plan.

Real-world applications of NVLM 1.0 in personalized tutoring and learning management systems are particularly noteworthy. The model can adapt to individual learning styles, offering tailored feedback and explanations based on the student's progress. It can help students understand difficult concepts by providing visual aids or answering questions that integrate both text and imagery. This adaptability is crucial in online education, where personalized attention is often limited.

Moreover, NVLM 1.0 can be used in automated grading systems, where it not only evaluates written responses but also interprets diagrams and images submitted by students. This reduces the administrative burden on educators and ensures that students receive more accurate and timely feedback, enhancing the overall learning experience.

Finance: AI in Accounting, Invoicing, and Fraud Detection

In the finance industry, time is money, and efficiency is paramount. NVLM 1.0's capabilities are streamlining many of the manual processes involved in accounting, invoicing, and fraud detection, making financial operations faster, more accurate, and more secure. By automating routine tasks and improving decision-making processes, AI models like NVLM 1.0 are reshaping the financial sector and setting the stage for a future where AI-driven automation is the norm.

One of the most impactful applications of NVLM 1.0 in finance is its ability to speed up data analysis for accounting professionals. The model can process invoices, receipts, and other financial documents—both text-based and image-based—much faster than a human ever could. It can automatically categorize expenses, detect discrepancies, and flag potential errors or fraudulent activity. This not only saves time but also reduces the risk of human error, ensuring greater accuracy in financial reporting.

Furthermore, NVLM 1.0 plays a critical role in fraud detection. The model's multimodal capabilities allow it to analyze transaction data, invoices, and other relevant documents to identify patterns that could indicate fraudulent behavior. By combining textual data, such as transaction records, with visual cues (like scanned receipts or signatures), NVLM 1.0 can provide a more holistic approach to detecting and preventing fraud.

Financial institutions can leverage these insights to safeguard against fraudulent activities and protect both businesses and customers.

The future of financial automation looks bright with AI models like NVLM 1.0 leading the charge. The automation of routine tasks such as data entry, invoice processing, and financial reconciliation will free up time for financial professionals to focus on more strategic initiatives. Additionally, AI models can predict market trends and assist in investment decisions by analyzing both structured and unstructured financial data. This is just the beginning of AI's transformative role in the finance sector.

Entertainment: AI in Content Creation

Entertainment is perhaps the most dynamic and creative industry to benefit from advancements in AI. NVLM 1.0 is revolutionizing content creation in a variety of ways, from scriptwriting and video production to advertising and personalized content generation. With its ability to process both text and visual data, NVLM 1.0 is opening up new creative possibilities, making it easier for content creators to produce high-quality material faster and more efficiently.

In scriptwriting and video production, NVLM 1.0 can be used to generate ideas, create drafts, and even assist in editing. For instance, the model can analyze a given script, offer suggestions for improvements, and help generate new dialogue or scenes based on the tone and style of the original content. By doing so, it accelerates the creative process and allows writers to focus more on storytelling rather than getting bogged down in the technical aspects of writing.

Moreover, NVLM 1.0 is revolutionizing advertising by enabling personalized content generation. Marketers can use the model to create targeted ads that appeal to specific demographics by analyzing consumer behavior and preferences. It can also help in creating dynamic ads that adapt based on the viewer's reactions or the context in which the ad is being shown. The result is more engaging and effective advertising campaigns that resonate with audiences on a deeper level.

Personalized experiences are another area where NVLM 1.0 excels. By analyzing a combination of text (such as user preferences) and visual content (such as images or video), the model can generate personalized recommendations or even create custom content. Streaming services, for example, can use NVLM 1.0 to suggest movies or TV shows based on a user's viewing history, while gaming platforms can generate custom levels or characters based on player behavior.

The impact of NVLM 1.0 on various industries is both profound and far-reaching. From transforming healthcare by improving diagnostics and patient care, to revolutionizing education with interactive and personalized learning experiences, NVLM 1.0 is reshaping the way businesses operate and create.

In finance, the model's ability to streamline data analysis and detect fraud is helping organizations stay ahead in an increasingly complex and fast-paced industry. Meanwhile, in entertainment, NVLM 1.0 is enabling more dynamic content creation, personalized advertising, and immersive consumer experiences. As AI continues to evolve, NVLM 1.0 will undoubtedly play a key role in the next wave of innovation, pushing the boundaries of what is possible and unlocking new opportunities across a wide range of industries.

Chapter 7: Understanding the Technical Marvel of NVLM 1.0

As AI continues to evolve, it's not just about the outcomes these systems can produce, but also about the intricacies of their design that make these advancements possible. NVLM 1.0, Nvidia's cutting-edge multimodal AI model, exemplifies the extraordinary capabilities that can emerge from combining innovation in architecture, training methodologies, and data handling. Understanding the technical framework behind NVLM 1.0 is crucial to appreciating how it's set to transform industries and lead the way for the future of artificial intelligence. This chapter dives into the hybrid architecture, training strategies, and image-processing techniques that distinguish NVLM 1.0 from other AI models.

The Hybrid Architecture of NVLM 1.0

At the core of NVLM 1.0 lies its hybrid architecture, a carefully engineered fusion of multiple design elements that makes it stand out in the crowded field of AI models. Unlike traditional models that rely heavily on one type of architecture, NVLM 1.0 blends the best of both worlds by combining decoder-only and cross-attention-based frameworks. This hybrid approach allows for superior training flexibility and enhances performance across a broad range of tasks, from natural language processing to visual data interpretation.

The decoder-only model, typically used in language models like GPT, is designed to excel in generating coherent text based on the input it receives. However, this architecture alone doesn't suffice when you're dealing with multimodal tasks that require integrating both text and image data.

To address this, Nvidia has incorporated cross-attention mechanisms into NVLM 1.0's architecture, allowing the model to focus attention on relevant parts of both the textual and visual inputs simultaneously. This ensures a more cohesive understanding of the relationship between the two modalities, making the model exceptionally powerful for tasks such as visual question answering (VQA), image captioning, and other vision-language fusion applications.

By merging the strengths of both these design elements, NVLM 1.0 can handle a range of complex tasks that single-modality models may struggle with. The hybrid architecture is crucial for improving accuracy and efficiency, allowing NVLM 1.0 to handle everything from simple textual queries to more complex scenarios that require reasoning based on visual and textual data in tandem.

Training NVLM 1.0: A Focus on Quality and Diversity

The training process of NVLM 1.0 is a meticulously designed venture that focuses not just on the sheer volume of data, but on the quality and diversity of the datasets used. While many AI models may rely on massive datasets to train their algorithms, Nvidia's approach goes a step further by ensuring that the data used in training is not only large but also relevant and diverse, maximizing the model's performance across different domains.

In traditional AI models, training often involves massive amounts of data scraped from the internet—datasets that are large in quantity but lack the specialized variety needed to address specific tasks. NVLM 1.0, on the other hand, focuses on the curation of datasets that are carefully tailored to enhance its multimodal abilities.

For instance, Nvidia ensures that the textual data used for training spans a variety of topics, genres, and contexts, so the model can better understand and generate nuanced responses. Similarly, the visual data—ranging from medical images to everyday objects—is diverse enough to cover different visual contexts, allowing the model to interpret a wide range of imagery and apply that knowledge to real-world scenarios.

By focusing on quality over quantity, NVLM 1.0 ensures that the model isn't just exposed to a massive amount of data but also to the right kind of data that helps it excel in both text and visual tasks. This balanced approach enables the model to understand intricate relationships between text and images, making it far more capable of handling complex queries that require insights drawn from both modalities.

Tile Tagging and Image Processing

One of the most innovative aspects of NVLM 1.0 is its ability to process high-resolution images more effectively than many of its competitors. Traditional image-processing models often face challenges when dealing with large or complex images. These challenges include issues with resolution, spatial understanding, and the computational cost of processing large image files. NVLM 1.0 addresses these issues with its unique use of a technique known as tile tagging.

Tile tagging is a process that involves breaking down an image into smaller, manageable sections—"tiles"—each of which is processed independently. This approach allows NVLM 1.0 to analyze high-resolution images more efficiently, as each tile can be processed with greater focus and accuracy. Instead of overwhelming the model with the entirety of a large image at once, the image is divided into smaller segments that are easier to process while retaining the full detail and context.

The real power of tile tagging lies in how NVLM 1.0 synthesizes these individual tiles back together to create a comprehensive understanding of the image. The model can focus on crucial details within each tile, while also being able to understand how these details fit into the broader context of the image. This ensures that even the most complex, high-resolution images—such as satellite images, medical scans, or detailed product photographs—are processed with exceptional accuracy.

This innovative image-processing technique is a key differentiator for NVLM 1.0, particularly when compared to other multimodal models that may struggle to efficiently handle high-resolution visual data. Whether in healthcare, where medical imaging requires high accuracy, or in other fields such as retail or manufacturing, NVLM 1.0's ability to process and understand complex visual data is a game-changer.

Real-World Applications of Tile Tagging in Visual Data Handling

The real-world applications of tile tagging in visual data handling are vast, with NVLM 1.0's efficiency offering significant advantages in industries where image analysis plays a crucial role. In healthcare, for example, the model's ability to process high-resolution medical images efficiently allows for faster diagnoses and more accurate results. Tile tagging enables NVLM 1.0 to process MRI scans, CT scans, and other detailed medical imaging with minimal computational overhead, making it an invaluable tool for doctors and radiologists.

Similarly, in industries like manufacturing, NVLM 1.0 can be used to analyze complex product images, detect defects, or verify quality assurance processes. By processing images piece by piece and understanding the relationship between different visual elements, the model can spot anomalies that may be invisible to the human eye, improving product quality and reducing operational costs.

In agriculture, tile tagging allows NVLM 1.0 to analyze satellite imagery or drone footage with greater precision, detecting issues like crop diseases or soil conditions across large areas. The model can identify patterns within these high-resolution images, enabling better decision-making for farmers and agricultural companies.

The ability to efficiently process and analyze high-resolution visual data is also valuable in the field of autonomous vehicles. NVLM 1.0 can be used to analyze images from multiple sensors and cameras, providing real-time decision-making capabilities for self-driving cars. The combination of text and visual data interpretation ensures that these vehicles can not only "see" their environment but also understand and respond to it intelligently.

The technical marvel behind NVLM 1.0 lies in its hybrid architecture, training methodologies, and advanced image-processing techniques, all of which contribute to its groundbreaking capabilities.

By combining the strengths of decoder-only and cross-attention designs, the model has redefined what multimodal AI can achieve. Its focus on quality and diverse data sets during training ensures that NVLM 1.0 can tackle real-world problems with an unmatched level of precision. Moreover, its innovative use of tile tagging for image processing provides a distinct advantage in handling high-resolution visual data, unlocking new possibilities across industries ranging from healthcare and manufacturing to agriculture and autonomous vehicles.

With these technical innovations, NVLM 1.0 is poised to set new standards for what AI can accomplish, opening the door to a future where

AI models are smarter, more efficient, and more capable than ever before.

Chapter 8: NVLM 1.0's Potential for the Future of AI

As we look toward the future of artificial intelligence, NVLM 1.0 stands at the precipice of transforming entire industries, setting a foundation for the next generation of multimodal AI models. Nvidia's latest creation isn't just an iteration of current AI systems—it represents a massive leap forward in what is possible when we bring together the realms of language, vision, and problem-solving. As AI continues to evolve, NVLM 1.0's multifaceted capabilities are primed to reshape the technological landscape, offering profound implications for both the near future and the decades ahead.

AI's Role in the Coming Decade

NVLM 1.0 is poised to play a pivotal role in the coming decade as it lays the groundwork for what will be seen as the next generation of artificial intelligence. While the past few years have seen significant advancements in AI models focused on specialized tasks—whether for language processing, image recognition, or problem-solving—NVLM 1.0 represents the intersection of these disciplines into a cohesive, multimodal framework.

In the coming years, we can expect AI to become increasingly integrated into everyday life, solving complex problems, assisting with decision-making, and augmenting human capabilities in ways we've never imagined. Healthcare, education, and entertainment are just a few of the sectors that will see exponential growth thanks to AI advancements like NVLM 1.0.

The ability of AI to process and understand both text and images is opening up new possibilities that will change how we interact with machines.

In healthcare, for instance, NVLM 1.0's capacity to analyze both medical records and diagnostic images can lead to more accurate and timely diagnosis. The AI will assist doctors in reviewing patient histories, interpreting medical scans, and even suggesting treatments based on vast data sets. In education, NVLM 1.0 can power personalized tutoring systems that understand students' individual learning needs, adapting lessons to match each student's pace and style of learning. Similarly, the entertainment industry will benefit from AI's ability to create more personalized content, from dynamic storytelling in video games to tailored recommendations in streaming services.

AI will no longer be just a tool used for specific tasks but an integrated part of daily life, supporting human ingenuity in ways that augment rather than replace our work. NVLM 1.0's groundbreaking design will serve as the model for future innovations in AI, where models continue to grow in complexity and sophistication, ultimately blending multiple types of intelligence to create even more capable systems.

The Long-Term Impact of Multimodal AI

The true significance of NVLM 1.0 lies in the way it represents the convergence of two powerful AI modalities—vision and language. While AI models have traditionally been either focused on processing text or images, NVLM 1.0's ability to handle both at the same time marks a major shift in AI development. This multimodal fusion is not just a trend—it is the future of artificial intelligence.

In a world where we interact with both textual and visual data simultaneously—whether in the form of videos, social media posts, product descriptions, or multimedia learning materials—AI models like NVLM 1.0 are uniquely positioned to understand and process these types of information together. This allows AI to operate closer to how humans naturally process and understand the world. As these models evolve, we may witness breakthroughs in how AI systems comprehend complex scenes, recognize nuanced human interactions, and provide more accurate responses to multifaceted questions.

The potential for multimodal AI models to uncover insights and generate solutions is staggering. Think of an AI system capable of synthesizing medical literature with patient imagery, instantly understanding both the symptoms and the context behind them to provide more comprehensive diagnoses. Or an AI that can read through educational material while analyzing accompanying visuals, creating a tailored curriculum for every student based on their individual learning patterns and real-time performance. These are just the starting points for the kinds of innovations we may see emerge from models like NVLM 1.0.

Furthermore, the true potential of multimodal AI may be much broader than we can currently imagine. With NVLM 1.0 leading the way, there will inevitably be breakthroughs and applications that haven't yet been thought of. As more data is fed into such models and their capabilities grow, AI could become an even more integral part of the solutions to some of humanity's most pressing challenges, from climate change to space exploration.

The Challenges Ahead

While the future of multimodal AI is incredibly promising, there are still many challenges that need to be addressed before we can fully unlock the potential of models like NVLM 1.0. One of the most significant hurdles is the ethical implications that come with such advanced technology.

With great power comes great responsibility, and as AI models become more intelligent and integrated into society, the risks associated with their misuse become more pronounced.

For instance, the ability of NVLM 1.0 to process vast amounts of visual and textual data raises privacy concerns, especially when it comes to sensitive information. How do we ensure that AI systems respect individual privacy while still performing their tasks effectively? Who has access to the data, and how is it used? These questions must be addressed as we continue to build more powerful AI systems, ensuring that safeguards are in place to protect users.

Another challenge is ensuring that AI models remain transparent, fair, and accountable. As AI systems become more autonomous, it becomes increasingly difficult to understand how they make decisions. This opacity can be problematic, particularly in fields like healthcare, finance, and law, where AI decisions can have significant real-world consequences. NVLM 1.0 and other future AI systems will need to evolve in a way that allows for greater transparency in their decision-making processes, allowing both users and developers to understand why a model made a particular recommendation or decision.

Finally, as AI systems like NVLM 1.0 become more powerful, there is the potential for job displacement and social disruption. While AI has the potential to significantly improve productivity and unlock new creative possibilities, it also threatens to automate many tasks traditionally done by humans. Policymakers, business leaders, and technologists must work together to ensure that the rise of AI does not leave individuals and communities behind. This could include rethinking education and job training, so workers can transition into new roles as AI changes the landscape of various industries.

As we look ahead, the potential of NVLM 1.0 to shape the future of artificial intelligence is enormous.

Its hybrid architecture, multimodal capabilities, and real-world applications are just the beginning of a broader AI revolution that promises to impact nearly every aspect of our lives. The long-term impact of this technology is hard to predict, but it is certain that multimodal AI like NVLM 1.0 will lead the way in fields ranging from healthcare to entertainment. However, with great power comes great responsibility. As we continue to innovate, it is essential to address the ethical, social, and transparency issues surrounding AI, ensuring that its advancements benefit society as a whole.

The future of AI holds tremendous promise, but it is up to us to shape it in a way that is responsible, fair, and inclusive for all.

Chapter 9: The Future of NVLM 1.0 and AI as a Whole

The rapid pace of artificial intelligence development has reshaped industries, transformed everyday life, and unlocked new potential for problem-solving. Nvidia's NVLM 1.0 has become a groundbreaking milestone in this evolution, setting the bar for future multimodal models that can handle both text and visual data with incredible precision. But as impressive as NVLM 1.0 is, its journey is far from over. In fact, the future of NVLM 1.0 and the AI landscape as a whole is ripe with possibilities, as the model's potential continues to grow and influence new areas of technology. The next chapter in the evolution of AI promises even greater innovation, opportunities, and challenges.

What Comes Next for NVLM 1.0?

As with all advanced technology, NVLM 1.0 will not remain static.

Nvidia is already pushing the boundaries of AI, and NVLM 1.0 is likely to see significant updates and improvements in the coming years. The underlying architecture of the model, which expertly integrates vision and language tasks, is only the beginning of what can be achieved. Future versions of NVLM may improve on the current model's speed, accuracy, and scalability, expanding its utility even further across industries.

One area where NVLM 1.0 may see enhancements is in the complexity of problem-solving tasks. While the current model excels in optical character recognition (OCR), visual question answering (VQA), and other core functions, future iterations may introduce more sophisticated problem-solving capabilities.

This could include even more advanced reasoning tasks or the integration of more diverse data sources, enabling NVLM to provide even deeper insights across various domains like law, medicine, and engineering.

Additionally, Nvidia may evolve NVLM to cater to a wider range of industries. For instance, while healthcare, education, and business applications are already well-supported by NVLM 1.0, future updates might enhance its adaptability to specialized industries such as manufacturing, logistics, or transportation. Integrating real-time data streams, for instance, could enable NVLM to assist in live decision-making for fields where timing and precision are critical.

Moreover, the evolution of the model could make NVLM even more accessible and customizable, allowing organizations to fine-tune its capabilities based on their specific needs.

By offering more flexible and user-friendly tools, Nvidia could further democratize the technology, enabling smaller businesses and independent developers to leverage NVLM's power for a broader array of applications.

How the AI Landscape Will Look Post-NVLM 1.0

The introduction of NVLM 1.0 marks a significant shift in the AI landscape, pushing the boundaries of what is possible with multimodal models. But what does the AI landscape look like in the wake of this groundbreaking technology? How will other companies and industries respond?

One clear trend that will emerge post-NVLM 1.0 is the increased focus on multimodal AI models. Nvidia's success with NVLM has proven that integrating text and vision tasks into a single model can dramatically enhance AI performance and open up new avenues of application.

As NVLM 1.0 continues to gain traction, other AI giants will be motivated to develop their own multimodal systems to compete. We will likely see an influx of research into hybrid models that combine different types of data—audio, video, and text—expanding the capabilities of AI even further.

Startups and independent developers will play a crucial role in shaping the future of this field. With Nvidia's open-source commitment, NVLM 1.0 could catalyze a wave of new innovations from smaller companies looking to build on the framework provided by Nvidia. These independent developers might apply NVLM to emerging sectors such as augmented reality (AR), virtual reality (VR), or autonomous vehicles, potentially expanding the scope of multimodal AI into even more groundbreaking applications.

However, Nvidia's breakthrough also sets the stage for fierce competition.

Other AI companies, like OpenAI and Google, will undoubtedly seek to match or surpass the performance of NVLM 1.0. Expect a race among AI giants to create the next generation of multimodal models—whether by refining their existing systems, integrating new types of data, or building more efficient models that can scale with growing demands. The rapid pace of technological development will ensure that the AI field remains dynamic and competitive.

The Road Ahead: Innovations on the Horizon

Looking further into the future, NVLM 1.0 represents just the first step in a much larger evolution of multimodal AI. As the AI field continues to mature, the next big leaps will involve integrating new and emerging technologies with NVLM's core framework. These innovations will not only enhance the capabilities of NVLM 1.0 but also provide broader insights into the potential of artificial intelligence.

One area where AI is already seeing rapid advancement is in neuromorphic computing, which seeks to mimic the way the human brain processes information. If Nvidia integrates neuromorphic chips with NVLM 1.0, the resulting hybrid could lead to a truly transformative AI system. This type of integration would allow for even more natural and flexible problem-solving capabilities, making AI systems more intuitive and adaptable.

Quantum computing is another emerging technology that could revolutionize AI models. While quantum computing is still in its infancy, its potential to process vast amounts of data simultaneously could dramatically speed up AI training times and increase the complexity of models like NVLM 1.0.

The combination of quantum computing with multimodal AI could unlock entirely new dimensions of capabilities, enabling the development of models that can handle unprecedented volumes of data and perform tasks that are currently unimaginable.

Finally, advances in natural language processing (NLP) will continue to push AI toward more sophisticated language understanding. While NVLM 1.0 already excels at combining language and vision, the ongoing refinement of NLP algorithms could allow NVLM to better grasp the nuances of human language, from slang and idiomatic expressions to complex sentence structures. This improvement will bring AI even closer to achieving human-like comprehension, enabling more accurate translations, more context-aware responses, and more personalized interactions.

In parallel, the integration of AI with other digital technologies—such as 5G networks, the

Internet of Things (IoT), and edge computing—will create opportunities for new AI applications. These innovations will enable faster, more efficient data processing, bringing real-time AI decision-making into areas like autonomous driving, smart cities, and personalized healthcare.

The Next Big Leap for AI in the Context of Multimodal Models

As the AI industry continues to progress, the next big leap will likely involve further refinement of multimodal models like NVLM 1.0. While current multimodal AI systems have made significant strides, the full potential of integrating text, vision, and possibly even audio and haptic feedback remains untapped. As the technology matures, we could see AI that not only understands text and images but also responds to environmental stimuli, emotions, and human interactions in real time.

Moreover, the ability to train models across multiple modalities simultaneously will likely pave the way for AI systems that can understand more complex relationships between different types of data. These advancements will lead to AI models that are even more intuitive, capable of providing richer insights, more accurate predictions, and more personalized recommendations in virtually every domain, from finance to entertainment.

The future of AI is bright, and NVLM 1.0 is just the beginning. As this technology evolves, we can expect new innovations to continue to reshape industries, enhance productivity, and offer transformative solutions to global challenges. With a solid foundation in place, the road ahead promises to be filled with groundbreaking advances that will unlock even greater potential for both AI and humanity.

Conclusion: The End of the Beginning

As we conclude our deep dive into Nvidia's NVLM 1.0, it's clear that the model represents a monumental step forward in the world of artificial intelligence. While this marks the end of one chapter, it is, in fact, just the beginning of what promises to be an exciting, transformative journey for AI technology. NVLM 1.0 has not only set new benchmarks but has also paved the way for the next generation of multimodal AI models that will shape the future of industries, research, and everyday life.

Summary of Key Takeaways

NVLM 1.0 stands out as a truly groundbreaking AI model, combining text and vision processing in a way that few others have managed.

Its architecture, which blends the best features of decoder-only and cross-attention-based designs, enables it to excel in a wide range of tasks, from optical character recognition (OCR) to complex problem-solving. The model's ability to seamlessly integrate these capabilities positions it as a game-changer in AI development.

One of NVLM 1.0's key strengths is its versatility. By overcoming many of the traditional trade-offs associated with multimodal AI, Nvidia has created a model that performs exceptionally well across both text and visual domains without compromising on accuracy or efficiency. It's no longer necessary to sacrifice one capability for the other, making NVLM 1.0 a prime candidate for real-world applications across industries like healthcare, education, business, and entertainment.

Perhaps even more significant is how NVLM 1.0 challenges the status quo.

Where previous AI models focused on text or vision separately, Nvidia's approach pushes the boundaries of what's possible by combining both modalities into a single, cohesive system. This approach doesn't just raise the bar in terms of performance but also challenges the way we think about AI—highlighting the potential for systems that can process and reason with multiple forms of data at once. In doing so, NVLM 1.0 sets a new standard for multimodal AI models that will influence future developments in the field.

The Bigger Picture

The release of NVLM 1.0 marks a significant shift in AI's trajectory. As powerful as the model is, its true impact is yet to be fully realized, and its capabilities are likely to evolve in the years to come. Nvidia's commitment to open-source AI and making NVLM 1.0 accessible to developers and researchers ensures that the technology will continue to grow and inspire innovation in countless fields.

The democratization of AI is a central theme in this story, with Nvidia providing the tools and platform necessary for even small startups and independent developers to harness NVLM's power and contribute to its evolution.

Looking ahead, the long-term implications of NVLM 1.0 extend far beyond its technical capabilities. This model represents a turning point in AI research and development, encouraging a more holistic approach to combining multiple data types and pushing the envelope on what AI can achieve. As AI continues to integrate more and more types of sensory data—whether that's audio, haptics, or environmental cues—models like NVLM 1.0 will serve as the foundation for future breakthroughs in human-computer interaction.

NVLM 1.0 also signifies a broader trend of accessibility and versatility in AI. As the model evolves, we can expect it to become even more adaptable and customizable, offering a wider array of tools for specific industries.

The potential for AI to serve not just as a tool but as a partner in solving complex, real-world problems is now closer than ever. Whether in healthcare, education, finance, or any other sector, NVLM 1.0 represents a model that can evolve with its users, meeting new challenges and unlocking untapped potential along the way.

What NVLM 1.0 Represents for the Future of AI: Innovation, Accessibility, and Versatility

Looking at NVLM 1.0 within the broader context of AI development, it's clear that the model embodies three key principles that will define the future of AI: innovation, accessibility, and versatility. Its groundbreaking combination of vision and text is an example of AI's potential to continuously innovate and push the boundaries of what's possible.

By making this model open-source, Nvidia is contributing to a more open, collaborative AI ecosystem, where innovation can come from anywhere, not just large corporations. This accessibility allows smaller companies, independent developers, and researchers to harness NVLM's capabilities, helping to level the playing field and drive further innovation.

Finally, NVLM 1.0's versatility is a testament to the future of AI systems that can solve complex, interdisciplinary problems. Rather than being limited to specific, narrow tasks, NVLM is designed to handle a wide array of tasks across multiple domains. This versatility ensures that as the technology evolves, it can adapt to new applications and contexts, helping to shape the future of industries, research, and technology in profound ways.

In conclusion, while NVLM 1.0 may represent the end of one stage in the AI revolution, it also marks the beginning of an exciting new era.

The model's capabilities are just the starting point, and its future development will continue to push the limits of what we know about AI and what it can achieve. From reshaping industries to unlocking new possibilities in AI research, NVLM 1.0 is not just a breakthrough in technology—it's a glimpse into the future of artificial intelligence.

Appendix: Resources for Researchers, Developers, and Innovators

The following appendix provides a comprehensive collection of resources to help researchers, developers, and innovators dive deeper into the world of NVLM 1.0 and artificial intelligence in general. Whether you're looking for tools to integrate NVLM 1.0 into your own projects, reading materials to expand your understanding of AI and multimodal models, or clarifications on common technical terms, this section will guide you toward the most relevant resources available.

Useful Links and Tools

How to Access NVLM 1.0 via Megatron Core

Megatron Core: Nvidia's Megatron Core is the platform that hosts and facilitates access to NVLM 1.0. Through this platform, you can explore the model's capabilities, test it on various tasks, and even integrate it into your own applications.

Accessing NVLM 1.0: For those looking to experiment with NVLM 1.0, it's essential to get started with Megatron Core, which provides all the necessary tools and infrastructure to run and manipulate the model.

Megatron Core Documentation – The official resource for setup instructions, API documentation, and model deployment.

Download NVLM 1.0 – How to get the model for testing, research, and development purposes.

Recommended AI Research Papers and Articles To understand the underlying theory and advances that power NVLM 1.0, here is a curated list of influential research papers and articles:

"Attention Is All You Need" (Vaswani et al., 2017) – The foundational paper on transformer models, which NVLM 1.0 builds upon.

"Multimodal Transformers for Image-Text Interaction" (Li et al., 2020) – This paper explains the fundamentals of combining vision and language in AI models.

"Megatron: Training Multi-Billion Parameter Language Models" (Shoeybi et al., 2020) – Focuses on the architecture of large transformer-based models and their training methodologies.

Nvidia's Research Blog – Stay updated with the latest advancements and applications in AI by reading Nvidia's official blog. It includes technical deep-dives into NVLM 1.0, as well as broader trends in AI research.

AI Model Evaluation Resources

AI Benchmarking Tools: To see how NVLM 1.0 compares to other models, it's important to use reliable benchmarking tools.

The Big AI Benchmark – A comprehensive evaluation platform for various AI models.

AI Model Performance Tools – A resource that allows users to track the latest benchmarks across multiple domains, including visual question answering (VQA), OCR, and language tasks.

Glossary of Terms

AI, machine learning, and multimodal models come with a complex set of terminologies that can sometimes be confusing. Below is a glossary of common terms, explanations, and their relevance to NVLM 1.0:

Multimodal AI: An artificial intelligence model capable of processing and integrating multiple types of data inputs (e.g., text, images, video) for decision-making and problem-solving.

Decoder-Only Architecture: A model design where the system primarily generates outputs based on input sequences, as opposed to encoder-decoder architectures that use both components for transforming input data into output.

Cross-Attention Mechanism: A mechanism in AI models that allows them to "attend" or focus on different parts of their input when generating outputs, especially in multimodal tasks like image captioning or visual question answering.

OCR (Optical Character Recognition): The AI task of converting images of text into machine-readable text. NVLM 1.0 excels at OCR by processing high-resolution images to recognize and extract text accurately.

VQA (Visual Question Answering): A task where AI models answer questions based on the content of an image. NVLM 1.0 demonstrates excellent performance on VQA, interpreting visual content and correlating it with textual queries.

Transformer: A type of deep learning model architecture known for its efficiency in processing sequential data (like language) and its ability to handle long-range dependencies in text.

Tile Tagging: A novel design in NVLM 1.0 for improving image processing. Tile tagging involves segmenting an image into smaller, manageable tiles for better recognition, especially for high-resolution visual data.

Megatron Core: Nvidia's platform used for training and deploying large AI models like NVLM 1.0, optimized for distributed computing across multiple GPUs.

Neural Network: A computing system inspired by the way biological brains work. It consists of layers of interconnected "neurons" that process data and make decisions. In the context of

NVLM 1.0, the neural network architecture underpins the model's ability to process both text and images.

Further Reading

For those interested in further expanding their knowledge in AI and multimodal models, we recommend the following books, articles, and courses:

Books

"Deep Learning" by Ian Goodfellow, Yoshua Bengio, and Aaron Courville: A classic textbook that provides in-depth explanations of neural networks, machine learning, and deep learning principles.

"Artificial Intelligence: A Modern Approach" by Stuart Russell and Peter Norvig: A comprehensive introduction to AI, covering its history, theories, and applications.

"Transformers for Natural Language Processing" by Denis Rothman: A focused guide on transformer architectures, perfect for those interested in understanding the model architecture behind NVLM 1.0.

Articles

"AI in the 21st Century: From Data to Insights" – An insightful article on the current and future implications of AI in various industries.

"Understanding the Impact of Multimodal AI on Modern Technology" – Explores how multimodal AI models, such as NVLM 1.0, are changing industries.

Online Courses

Coursera – Deep Learning Specialization (Andrew Ng): A comprehensive series of courses that covers the foundations of deep learning and neural networks, which form the backbone of models like NVLM 1.0.

edX – Artificial Intelligence: Implications for Business Strategy: A course offered by MIT that examines the strategic implications of AI technologies, focusing on practical applications and opportunities in business and tech.

Fast.ai – Practical Deep Learning for Coders: A hands-on deep learning course designed for developers, offering practical knowledge on creating AI models with real-world applications.

With these resources, you can dive deeper into the nuances of NVLM 1.0, multimodal AI, and the broader landscape of artificial intelligence. Whether you're a developer seeking to integrate NVLM 1.0 into your project, a researcher exploring new frontiers in AI, or a tech enthusiast eager to learn more about the future of AI, these tools and references will guide you along your journey.